Table of Content

MW01173702

EUGENIA

Ethical also

Uniquely

Genuine

Emotional, yet never

Naive

Impatient, however always

Achieved

Mysteriously

Intelligent

Ruler

Amazingly

Notorious, also

Divinely

Awesome

Justifiably

Amazing

Melanated

Empress

Sister

~U GenUis~

The Tree In Me

Dead on the inside but the outside still stand

Standing on dry land

Receiving rain

That causes pain

But yet that tree still remain

Planted

Rooted

In the ground

Leave those around

Hearing a whispering sound

Wondering what is that toneless sound that's heard

Very different from the sound of a mockingbird

Yet singing much needed words

Making needed shade with my leaves

Asking everyone to please stay with me

Allow me to protect you in this state of emergency

Allow my leaves to be an umbrella, keeping you dry

From the tears that you try to hide

No matter the amount of rain because my leaves spreads wide

My roots are rooted with land made soil

Able to withstand any forms of turmoil

Just like when barbecuing, you want the heavy duty foil

It keeps the food all warm and all

Just like this tree that refuses to fall

Even when the leaves die and the limbs break and falls

Seeming to the eyes to be weak

When the the sound of that tree starts to creek

It still holds shades of protection as we gather to speak

This tree…ohhh baby this tree

Has strength even when deadened…that tree is me

~U GenUis~

LISTEN

Come sit for a minute and let me talk to you

Know that you are amazing...quite outstanding, if I may say so

Let me tell you of the things that the world don't want you to know

You were designed to be a blessing, to conquer this life on Earth

See, just like me, some of us were scarred from birth

Understand that what you see as pain

Was designed to strengthen you, so stay sane

Allow your beauty to shine from within

Know that we ALL sin

You have to try everyday to be a BETTER you...DON'T PRETEND

Allow your natural light to shine, for it can't be dimmed

Shine baby...shine in front of all of them

Enjoy yourself everyday...smile, you are the star of the film

Your life is yours

You will make bad choices and wrong detours

Truth is, although you may fall...with God you shall stand

Stand firm as a palm tree when the hurricane hits the land

It's a valuable lesson to learn to back down and FOLLOW God's plan

For sure He got the plan if He can provide water to the dry land

You will experience some things done to you by man

THIS pertains to every man or woman

I'm not sure how you're feeling today but I've known this to be true

NOW...whatever you do

KEEP GOD FIRST,

NEVER LOSE YOURSELF

AND DON'T GIVE UP ON YOU

~U GenUis~

Faith When Hurt

Hurting…

Carrying burdens

Holding in

The Spirit that gives loneliness

But yet you have to remain peaceful and remember the obedience of forgiveness

Dealing with the mentality of separation to not feel finessed

Pulling and pulling to find your joy while holding your peace

Planting your feet on the ground because these winds are tossing you from west to east

Desiring to get closer to God so that you can feel His presence when your Spirit is at war

Making you dodge hurt due to the mental destruction from afar

Getting ready for battle with no weapons needed

But the word of God that never gets defeated

One thing about My God, He fights to the end

Which is why when He walks in front of you, you always win

Winning in the form of blessings that allows a new life to begin

But when you get this new life, what do you do

Do you remember the hardship in gaining faith after all that you've gone through

~U GenUis~

PROTECTING MY PEACE

Fighting for happiness in place so dark

Holding my peace so that anger don't spark

It's always bad when I start to speak

Trying to hold my tongue is not for the weak

Nor for the depressed

That seems to stress

Over the things that have made you so blessed

Mentally going back

To the past pain is so damn wack

It irritates my soul

When I'm trying to feel whole

Feels like these ppl are taking me into a dark hole

Fighting depression

Is not as easy as suppression

Then comes anxiety with all of the aggressions

That life has placed back in my view, now here comes the oppression

Do I stop where I'm at or stay afloat

Do I still have the strength to row this boat

But hey…that's another note

In the closed chapters that I tote

Being singled out…maybe just pushed to the side

Is a part of why I choose to not speak on what the next person feel I hide

When I'm happy, I want to smile

It's hard to get here…100 miles

Or maybe more like a million

That's why I choose to give no fucks about one's opinion

Judge yourself before you judge me

Maybe then you'll see

What it takes to smile and have a great day

Unfortunately all is seen is the work after I pray

I pray for strength to have joy in the midst of a world of pains

But looked at weird because I choose to leave pain as pain to remain sane

This is the main reason that I am me and you are you...we are not the same

~U GenUis~

Questioning

You are a weakness to my heart, yet makes my mind strong

You've been my glue when I'm shattered and feel I don't belong

My joy when angered and want to run away

Even when my mind goes, my soul still stay

Sleepless nights

When we have a verbal fight

Missing you…no matter who's wrong or right

Tossing and turning desiring you near

Your voice before I sleep is the sweetest sound to my ears

Comforting the loneliness that has for so long been my fear

Sometimes wondering…Am I in too deep here?

Or am I just afraid…fearful of pain

Of being hurt again and again

Pushing you back at the very sight

Of love, not knowing if it's wrong or right

Yet tormenting myself because, the feelings I feel, I fight!

~U GenUis~

Heavy Mind

My mind is blank and it's difficult to write.

I'm hurt but happy in the same light

Emotional yet stronger than normal

Due to hurt, pains and simple turmoil

Many see my strength but not my pain

Only because the world would hurt me over and over again

It took a near death experience

To make me mentally coherent

Enough to swallow the torment

I forgave

Yet it never saved

Me, no matter how I behaved

Blindsided from the roads that's been paved

In God I trust

Had become a must

To help me mentally adjust

Also accept

That I was kept

Only Because Jesus wept

His stripes healed my health

While strengthening my heart

That no one can tear apart

Only give me motivation to restart

My happiness and allow love to enter my heart

I yearn to be loved …that's something I need

Just like a baby that breastfeed

Love is the main ingredient…yes indeed

I give but can't receive

Love, however I must achieve

The honor of it all

Because God gave me a strength and smile that won't allow me to fall

~U GenUis~

LIES

Lies…is everyone's weakness

Whether it's intentional or just out of distress

Sometimes we tend to love the lie so bad

That we smile in joy of someone else being sad

Never realizing how it makes you mad to receive the same feelings…now look who's sad

Then boom we scream for loyalty

Not seeing our own disloyalties

But wait, some have the ability

To actually

Keep their loyalty

Regardless of what the circumstances may bring

Expecting the same energy we bring

Believing the mere words

That's heard

From your mouth, every word

Some of them are very obscured

Leaving the mentality disturbed

Now you don't understand why I choose to use the "F" word

~U GenUis~

MY HAPPY PLACE

Wishing I had a place

That takes the feeling of being misplaced

Something like a happy space

Allowing myself to write

Any time of the day or night

When I'm weary or needing some insight

Some time to examine myself

Trying to stop the feeling of needing mental help

See while most people problems comes from relationships

When there cheating, abuse...mentally and physically wanting to dip

Yeah...some of y'all are a whole trip

But see me, my fight is within my Soul

Trying to remain whole

In a world where holding a smile have become the ultimate goal

Afraid to become too weakened, so you fight to be strong

Even when finding it hard to hold on

Like to master holding on without gaining hate

Hate will keep you from Heaven's gates at the fastest rate

Still not understanding why so much weight

On a solid glass, yet paper feeling plate

Praying and praying

Crying to lay down and pray again

Because God is your ONLY way of relief, He is not a fashion trend

~U GenUis~

Around Here

Listening to the sound of gunshots ring

Not knowing what's happening

Dropping to the floor

Away from the windows and door

Not knowing if this city is safe for me anymore

No police sirens are heard

Not even the chirping of a bird

The law enforcements not even coming…this is absurd

It's the middle of the day

When the kids normally play

But yet they stray

All because of this senseless gun play

WHEN WILL THIS STOP…WHEN WILL THIS END

WHEN WILL BLACK MEN STAND UP AND TAKE BACK OUR CITY AGAIN

Bring the love, bring the joy

Show these young men the difference in a man and a boy

Show our young women that this road don't have to be lonely

Stand up and hold the fort…allow vulnerability

Teach our young ladies respect even when she feels unworthy

SHOW THIS WORLD HOW THAT STRENGTH IS STILL IN THE BLACK COMMUNITY

It's the strength of a man that's instilled in his voice box

There's much more to being a man other than a beard and a head of lox

When the black man speaks, his voice is heard

His tone don't have to be loud…not even one word

Women smile upon the sound of the black man's voice

There's comfort in knowing that you made the right choice

The choice to move…TAKE ACTION…MAKE A STAND

IT'S TIME FOR THIS WORLD TO SEE CHANGE AND KNOW THERE IS NOTHING ON EARTH GREATER THAN THE BLACK MAN!

~U GenUis~

Pushing forward

In these times we stand ashamed

Due to a name

That have made our generation become weakened and ashamed

Ashamed to be the color of our skin

The COLOR that made mankind begin

The COLOR that became hated yet adored

Adored by the same people that knocked us to the floor

YEAH, even looked at as poor

Not even worthy of the opening of a door

Never realizing we have the strength to move mountains

Because WE have been made for the rain

That produce pains

But yet we remained sane

WHY???….because it's time for a change!

But HOW do we change when the generations are restrained

MENTALLY before PHYSICALLY put into padlocked chains

Do we fall weakened to the streets and fall into the hands of the legal man

Or do we stand shoulders back and heads up, while birthing a plan

Not just any plan but a definite way

A way To regain our strength each everyday

To take back what they say

We didn't deserve anyway

But see We've struggled plenty of days, huh..huh, yeah you too!

Feeling down because the world seems to be against you

Looking into your own life and owning your own truths

This is what makes…ha ha you a greater you

When Will we one day open our own eyes to see that the reality might just be

That it's nothing but ourselves standing between you and me

Standing without standards

Wondering why the road is so tough

See our own people on billboards,

Looking for the killer, yeah that's rough

But We fight to be seen

We fight to be heard

Not realizing

It's really us against the world

It's you and I that stands in our way

The way we treat each other each everyday

The way we see each other

The words we say about one another

Do you build your fellow man

Do you give them a hand

Do you offer to be a chair if they can't stand

Are you prepared to love and not hurt

Or will it take seeing your like kind in the dirt

Are you comfortable living, still within the days of slaves

Are you ok living in caves

No..NOT me and don't tell me how to behave

When the way of this world keeps us enslaved

I'm not going back, I see the sun-rays   ~U GenUis~

In My City

In my city, it's a struggle from day to day

Where dying have become the only way the family pray

The only way we find time to love one another

To unite TOGETHER as sisters or brothers

These tears we cry on the next one's shoulders

Turns right around and become a mockery when the pain gets older

In my city, we'd rather see our fellow man hunger

Looking for a way to survive and help those that's younger

Seeing the next person struggle in your same footsteps

Yet we'll hush, while watching them sink into the lowest depths

Shaking our heads,

But yet claim to be Spirit led

Living but watching these youngsters come up dead

In my city, we'll join a force to drive a person insane

Not concerned of the mental pain

We just like internet fame

Yea…thats real lame

Better yet…The fact that we claim

To love one another, I'm guessing that's the game

Deeply envying the life of the next

Not realizing that God gave you what's for your best

In my city, pain becomes the new joy

Relationships are unreal and you can't tell the difference in a girl or boy

Everyone in life nowadays is a decoy

We challenge the real but accept the fake

We backstab one another...and scream STAY AWAKE

We promote what's bad, yet can't come together for the good

BUT SHREVEPORT, WE ARE SHREVEPORT...NO MATTER WHAT HOOD!

~U GenUis~

\

These Ole Shoes

To walk a walk that my shoes can't stand

Even when wearing the most expensive shoe in demand

Looking back on when I walked on shaky land

Yes shaky because even I didn't think I could withstand

Without the help of another hand

See, even when my troubles grew like feet

Like when the shoe and the tip of your toe finally meet

Causing me to some days, having to pause and take a seat

Having to reset and replete

Thinking and contemplating as I eat

But when those shoes got too small

Because remember, we can't take them all

Even prosperous stores have to close in the shopping mall

Giving the assumption that fashion is about to fall

Yet you get a new store like you get a new pair

Of shoes that has no despair

Of what might be ahead that's flown from the air

Don't let me lose you…stay right there

Allow me to tell you about when my feet grew from that pair

That walks through this life of unasked for pains

Always remaining sane

On this mentally, physically yet, emotional train

That seems to put weight on my membrane

I've learned to walk with bare feet

In any temperature of any heat

Learning when to retreat

Nevertheless always in defeat

Because I have steal feet

Feet that I use to walk with today and I'm asked how

My only response is... FEET DON'T FAIL ME NOW!

~U GenUis~

STILL WORTHY

Humbled yet destroyed from my soul

No…I don't feel whole

Feels like I'm crawling out of a deep hole

Holding my pains

That becomes mental strains

On my brains

But the world EXPECTS me to stay sane

Damn, how do I get off this train

That's flying and I don't know the destination

Loosing my breath, trying to slow down my respirations

Slowly breathing…feeling my heartbeat in my ear

Crying silent tears

So that no one knows I'm in fear

Head pounding but yet I'm stuck right here

How do I get off…how do I let go

Of the hurt, the pains…so that my feelings won't show

Allowing others to see how to knock me to the floor

Which is why I choose the room with the steal door

Where I can close off and no one have the opportunity to hurt me anymore

Realizing that some people don't deserve the good in me

One wrong turn and there is a shift of energy

Giving me the clear reality

That love and loyalty

Is not in my destiny

Only those that's quick to give up and turn a cold shoulder to me

Right when I gained the confidence to know that I am worthy

~U GenUis~

Shemothy

Ten percent is what you gave me

But I gave you pure loyalty

Without asking…I gave you the best of me

Yet when my pains arrive

You show so much pride

That you can't stop your stride

To see the hurt I'm holding inside

I cry…I text

But you treated me like the next

Simple bitch from the projects

You became numb

Now I feel dumb

Like a piece of chewed, tasteless gum

Mannn…this shit is fucking with my nerves and my income

I'm feeling weakened inside

But these feelings I must hide

Somehow and some where it seems I have lost my pride

Got my soul feeling fried

Yet, you don't and probably will never see

The true person in me

You will only remember the one day I had bad energy

I've given every form of apology

Even damn near begged you to be a shoulder for me

Lord…just give me mercy

I'm holding

Yet my soul is folding

Molding

Feels like a computer when it's decoding

Wanting the keys to stop pressing on me

But fuck!!!...this shit is fucking with my energy

Now I gotta be on my bad bitch shit

Know that it's me...UGENUIS ...THAT'S IT

AND YOUR TEN PERCENT AINT ENOUGH TO FUCK WITH THIS

I AM HER...I AM NO SIMPLE BITCH

~U GenUis~

WINE

Wine, wine, wine...ladies favorite cool out drink, right

We drink that wine and every stress of the day is completely out of sight

Some prefer dry wine, they like the roughness

Nothing like a lil roughneck to take away the toughness

When she gets that Cabaret

Her mind is then ready to play

Play but not ready to stay

For the night and day

Wine oh wine, I may not want to taste something so tough

Can you pass me the Zinfandel, see if its just sweet enough

Just a little but not much

There's a specific taste that i don't want to touch

Yes, you're just as smooth asPennsylvania Dutch

Not too strong,however, not too sweet

Just strong enough to strike a little heat

Red wine, I can't pass you up

Its times I have to specifically need you in my cup

Did I say cup...I meant glass

I do still have class

However, I might just take a pass

But wine oh wine...Moscato i see you

You sometime sparkle at me, but why you do me like you do

You have me smiling way too soon

You taste good to me but have me sleep til noon

Have me so relaxed

Ohhhh what a mental climax

Wondering can i afford this everyday, plus tax

Looking at myself in the mirror trying to see

Just which one of yall are really made for me

Got me searching my mental

Stopping myself from feeling all gentle

Only because of wine...

Wine is fine

But see me, I prefer Cognac, most of the time

~U GenUis~

Feeling Complete

Afraid, yet happier than I've ever been

Holding every fear and tear in

Praying without ceasing

That we start a new beginning

Building what was once destroyed within me

As well as the broken or bruised pieces of you

Knowing that you need me just like I need you

In reality, we need each other…no myth, straight truths

You're comfort to my mind

I trust you if my sight left me and I was blind

Trusting that you would never leave the needs and security of my heart behind

Never thought I'd meet a Lion that treat me so gentle and kind

I didn't even believe that true happiness was mines

Until you walked in my home and my strength declined

As in I had encountered MY King! The one specific man I've prayed for

I tried to deny that my strength hit the floor

So I ran from you because I have never felt that feeling before

Running but couldn't go far because it wasn't a magic door

However…it was a magnetic force that pulled on me

Every time I looked at you, the attraction…omg …on me

Like you read my soul, not just felt a vibe, you see

You could see me from my emotional, sensitivity

Even the empowered, strong woman…that's my normal category

Which is why my heart melts for you and that's so scary

I'm becoming softer…more gentle

Less stress is on my mental

I can be a woman ONLY, with you, I'm no man and this is true

I find myself really needing you

Desiring you

Yearning for you

Wanting to be in the hands of YOU

I feel I can be honest and say I'm afraid to loose you

Not to sound weakened but I am with you

I don't want to sound vulnerable but you allow that too

I can only be honest when I say these things to you

You complete me and I don't want to go back to the days that I didn't have you

~U GenUis~

SOUL CRY

Ever wanted to cry but the tears had no resting place

So in your soul you hold them and trace and retrace

Thru the thoughts...the pains

The loneliness and pressure of blood running thru my veins

Often wondering, am I made of steel

Am I not supposed to heal

Am I not supposed to feel

But holding because I know that God is real

Family in the same city

But I'm looked upon real shitty

Because I speak on how I feel yet, they are portrayed to be saditty

Camouflaging their realities

But seem to see nothing but the worst in me

Reaching out

But still there are doubts

Really getting tired of taking this same route

Taking the same streets

Feels like no treat

Just a break in my heartbeat

From the energy that's given feels like unextinguished heat

Taking me to my knees, off my feet

Why my knees...why not

What do you do when the mind feels shocked

When the heart feels cold

When your emotions are burning like hot coal

Do you pray, do you fold

I say move on with God...He is more valuable than a treasure hidden with diamonds and gold

~U GenUis~

VIBE

The desire to be loved from the depths of my soul

The part that keeps me mentally, spiritually, emotionally whole

The desire to laugh and also cry

The part of your heart that stops deceit…plain lies

The urge to protect me at any cost

I don't want your life…just be a Queen's boss

Wanting the best of me as I desire the best in you

Seeing my soul through my eyes, feel my emotions from my Spirit through and through

The emotional attachment to my daily energy

The glow in your eyes when you look at me

Allow me to smile and my heart to be free

Helping me to see, even when I'm blinded, that happiness is in my destiny

Tell me I'm beautiful on my worst days

When I feel weakened and cry, your help shouldn't be delayed

As I will keep you first, for your strength I'll pray

Vibe ole Vibe, is that you I'm feeling, by the way?

~U GenUis~

Being Rebuilt

Having nothing left but God and God alone

Sometimes makes the heart not feel so strong

Makes you feel weakened and defeated by all means

Not realizing this is life, we're all human beings

Human beings that God created piece by piece

Humans that depends on Him for an increase

An increase in love and pure understanding

Understanding how to hold when the planes skips its landing

Landing in a field where there's flowers with no bees

Alone with The Lord under that beautiful shade tree

Giving Him all hurts, pains and reasoning of wanting to let go

Y'all don't feel me huh, but one day you will for sure

For sure you will lay down to pray because kneeling seems to not be enough

But ooooh baby when your rise, Satan can't touch your type of tough

Toughness that stand thru sickness and in health

Toughness that makes you fight back for YOURSELF

~U GenUis~

I'm Blessed

Dying while alive is the most challenging thing to do

Trying to figure out why the world seems to say fuck you

Household in turmoil and everything seeming to fall

Attitudes on spike…making me want to take a hike

A hike in the woods alone with just my FATHER and I

Trying to get more insight and not physically die

Dying is easily done when the fights seems so frowned upon

Aiming to find strength when weakened because at this moment I feel defeated

Defeated because at this moment, right now, I feel my fight can't be defeated

HOWEVER, realizing I'm walking with the MAN and me…He will not leaveth

On this journey I saw my strength while defeating my weaknesses

I also learned that giving in when it's too heavy makes me nothing less

Nothing less than next person, I'm actually overly blessed

~U GenUis~

Grandmas

Grandmothers are the glue that secure the soul

The ones that holds the strength that's untold

The ones who cries

Cries every emotion out of their eyes

The prayers of the blessings that we see in disguise

Never knowing who talked to God and ask Him for favor

Realizing it came from Grandma...or maybe Grandpa whose love never waivered

They never walked away nor turned their backs on you

Even when you were angry and act like you do

Showing that love can be unmeasurable through and through

Seeing your flaws but never put up barricaded walls

Leaving themselves ALWAYS open to call

Love them and care for them like i love mines, THAT'S ALL

~U GenUis

Healing Smile

Just like a rose, a smile is not just a smile

Quite appealing and some can embrace it for quite a while

Some are made and held through countless amounts of deceit

Knowing that it only takes one wrong encounter before you drop to your feet

Just like a rose that comes in many colors

Some are solid but there's mixtures in others

Some come back and some stay away

Kinda like how your smile can change with the day

Some change in seconds, rather minutes

In most cases you can see their strength will start to diminish

If only you could see or feel

The emotions of that smile, will

Just will you take the time to help it heal

~U GenUis~

Just Thinking

Acknowledging who I am

In the midst of a world of scams

Making sure my life don't end up in a jam

Thanking God for my fam

Loving the mental intimacy

Asking God for those twins…Grace and Mercy

To continue to protect the vulnerability

That lies within me

Thanking God for showing my frenemies

As well as the "too good" people I'm my family

Those are the ones that's too blind to see

The true reality

And Woman of Stone God created in me

YES!!!…Woman of Stone

But I dare to be alone

Although my closet hearts is gone

You feel where I'm coming from

From a place of hurt

That seems to keep me alert

Thank God for my people in the dirt

~U GenUis~

Judgement

The finest wine sits years on reserve

Every grape is examined and crtitquly observed

The best ones are put into the pot

Judged by every indenture, every lump, any signs of rotten

Judged by the color it holds, the sweetness within

They're touched and felt on to make sure they are valuable, right

Forgetting to acknowledge the smaller ones, not to judge by sight

Even judged by the juices that flows, the dry ones never win

Can't forget those, the ones that's misfit…some missing skin

Some have dents

And some just don't mix

Even the dry ones get a place, they become raisins

Yet, still being judged by their skin

~U GenUis~

Strength To Stand

Learning to stand

When the presence of a man

Become your least command

Building your strength

Going through the longest miles…most distant length

Receiving strength that you can't resent

Nor can you deny that GOD…yea God is the one to honor

Just like they do the blood donors

When they are the most needed blood owners

Learning when to let go

Letting go of what's not there anymore

Yet, keeping your feet grounded to the floor

From relationships

To family and friendships

Know when it's time to dip

Be acrobatic and do a mental flip

Standing up for your worth

Is sometimes harder than a teenager giving birth

Yes…like bringing a child to Earth

Gives you the rare reality

That we come with no warranty

Yet strive to have a great destiny

With the mentality

To be all that you can be

Smiling

Not wilding

Praying

Not straying

From your knees to laying

Laying face down

Releasing all hurts and frowns

Knowing that there is a for sure blessing that coming around

Blessings in the form of joy, not pains

That heals the soul and makes sane of the insane

Allowing peace

To be the release

Of pressure to the brain

~U GenUis~

Searching

If pain was a person, I'd be HER!

From emotional detour

To love that's impure

Feelings of loneliness makes the pain mental

While this definitely impairs my physical

Yet, it all seems theatrical

Because this leads to pain that's Spiritual

Needing a ear

To hear

The difference between a smile and a tear

Also acknowledging the fear

Of emotionally leaving here

Someone to understand that I'm not suicidal, I will never hurt me

I'm a woman that deals with life indefinitely

Can't leave out INDEPENDENTLY

Thru sickness and pains

I pray to stay sane

Also for joy to remove these chains

That was placed to drive me insane

Praying for peace in my life and joy in my soul

I'm tired of the down days, I just want to feel whole

~U GenUis~

Always Grateful

Thanking God for my good while being grateful for my bad

Realizing that my life is a blessing that some have never had

Yes,

There has been times that I didn't feel too blessed

Simply thought of my life as a mess

Not realizing that God puts His strongest soldiers through the toughest test

It took some time for me to reset

Be thankful and never forget

Nor regret

The pains I've experienced because yet

I wasn't man made so man can't break me

The person within me had to face the rare reality

That God saw fit to see the very best in me

Which is why I Give Him all the glory

For never dimming the light on that diamond in the rough…lil ole me

Remembering those days when I felt defeated because my mind wouldn't let me win

Those days when I didn't see the beginning to think of an end

The times my struggle was greater than my hustle

When the bills and food wanted to tussle

Yea to win that fight, took every muscle

While fighting depression

Was my biggest lesson

~U GenUis~

My Thoughts

My thoughts, my thoughts…my motherfucking thoughts

Thinking about the trials… the tribulations and things I've been taught

The way I've reached out but only grabbed air

The days when I wanted to explode and no one was there

What about the jobs I've encountered and the people I've met

Realizing I still haven't found my ONE yet

Intimacy is a feeling that my mind haven't processed so I seem to forget

How it feels to be folded like an omelet

Thoughts of the ways I've and acted…some not too good

In some people eyes, I might seem to be hood

Truth is I'm the realest…let's get that understood

Although there have been times where my bad outweighed my good

Yet I stood firm like a palm tree's wood

Taking life and it challenges and eating them up

Drinking pain in a glass, don't give me no cup

Don't give me no sympathy because that's something I don't do

Just give me to God to be made anew

To forget about my past as He casts my sins from me

For strength to trust Him to stand up to my enemies

To take my stress and completely let go

To enjoy my blessings from the seeds I seem to sow

~U GenUis~

At First Sight

Do you believe in love at first sight

Do you think the timing could ever be so right

That you can find your soulmate without a fight

Like is this unexplainable feeling something real

Can you be the one person that God created to help me heal

As well as allow myself to feel

Yes, this is a big ordeal

Making me smile as I look at you

Is what I read in your eyes really true

If so,

you know

That I feel I was waiting on you

Or maybe it's that my loneliness

In silence has created a whole mess

Within me but wait…it's no stress

Because I will never, ever press

Anyone to see my best

All I have is me and my word

To some, my actions, too might hurt

But it's clearly because I dodge unhappiness like a butch dodges a skirt

If you can't enhance my smile

I'm willing to wait awhile

For the one that I can one day walk hand in hand with down the aisle.

I refuse

To be used

Or have my heart abused

Just so you can be amused

I'm worth every fight

Deserving of being your spotlight

Not just something that fly by night

But when you met me, you knew this, right?

~U GenUis~

Lost Vibe

Being fooled by a vibe that was accompanied by a smile

Lost, dreaming a dream I thought I saw through your sparkling eyes

Thoughts of being in this person's daily life…whew chile

Try opening up from your innermost needs

Your wants, your hurts and the desires of which your heart bleeds

Maybe it's just the thought that this certain type of joy could be a daily feel

Unfortunately, it's not, at some point I will have to heal

From the feeling of loneliness when you push me away

Knowing in my heart I want to beg you to stay

But I'm way too G

To be so weak and beg a person to see the best in me

Due to the simply fact that I know I'm worthy

So losing me is your lost, not mines

This, you will see in due time.

~U GenUis~

Fly Away

Mind in the clouds floating in the sky

Thinking if I had wings like a butterfly

How high would I fly

Does my destination stop when the load gets lighter

Do it mean I'm on the better end of life because my days seems brighter

Wiggling out of spots that seems to be getting tighter and tighter

Thinking of the days when I can't get a break

Times I felt like wet leaves on a rake

Acknowledging the strength it took to shake

The bad days that I thought I couldn't take

Trying God for myself was my best decision

Praying to block the pain and release the vision

Of hurt, disgust, neglect and mental division

While sitting in the background

Yet I'm still found

Trying to be in disguise

But I hold a light I couldn't hide

Never have I ever been the one to dick ride

Your life is your life and mines is mines

Just because I don't see life your way, I'm still not blind

It's never been a day you could question my grind

Even at the times

I wish to rewind

My past days to learn from any lesson's agenda, the lessons I didn't find   ~U GenUis~

In My Mind

I write this poetry to clear my mind

Clearance of the things that would make sight of the blind

Some of this just shit be too tough

Then there's the things that makes it seem like I don't struggle hard enough

Days that's been rough

Laughter that made me cry

The jokes that surrounds me so that my joy don't die

Thoughts of the times I wish I could fly

Out of situations that I thought was too hard to try

Aiming to be better than I was before

Wondering…do they make strong men anymore

Men that want to love you and restore

And sweep the hurts and pains off the floor

You know those type that do more than just hold the door

The type of men that see beauty in more forms that the eyes can see

The ones that see my imperfections and will still see the best in me

The men that desire a one man's woman

Not the type of woman that keep the drama coming

A woman that sees more in him than where he stands

A woman that help build him to becoming a stronger man

Do men want what's good,

Yet afraid or maybe just misunderstood

Do women expect more

Than men are willing to give anymore

Is real love and trust in relationships really a thing

If not…just take me back to when it was real from the beginning

~U GenUis~

The Depths of Me

In the depths of me, You will find a language that requires a translator

Just like when buying your dream home, you search for the highest rated realtor

A language that although it may be studied, it takes more to achieve

However the reward that's received

Is better than when a child is conceived

It's felt, not just told nor does it leave

I was born this way…this type of loyalty…

Don't come often

It makes the hardest heart soften

Releasing an energy that can't be forgotten

Regardless of how your heart has been hardened

My Spirit speaks right through my soul

Holding a strength that does not fold

Warming the temperature of a heart so cold

Emotionally speaking the untold

Releasing a vibe that consoles

Knowing I'm deserving of the best

Nothing but the best…I'm different from the rest

Desiring to feel a love so secure like the chest

When you put on that bullet proof vest

As well as the opportunity to push you to be your best

Knowing that BEHIND every strong man, there is stronger woman

Although humbled by your strength, I know when to stand

As well as when to hold because you are by far a real man

But see, there is a deeper part of me, please understand

In the depths of me

I desire to be

Loved correctly

Knowing I am deserving to be a great man's wifey

One that would love and cherish me

Release my past pains and destroyed energy

One that builds with me

That heals with me

Pray with me…

Yeah…you feel me

The ONE man designed JUST for ME

One that make me WANT to react submissively

The ONE that's been PREPARED and REPAIRED…as well as, gives me back to me

Because one thing for certain…when I get him, he will have all of me…

Love, honor, and respect…Genuinely

~U GenUis~

EMOTIONAL STORMS

My heart is aching an unexplainable pain

Thunder in my heart…tears like rain

Seems like this wind is brewing a category 5 hurricane

Feeling emotionally drained

Yet…remaining sane

Rebuilding myself and restoring what's been harmed

By this emotionally damaging…cold snow storm

Feeling frozen in my days

Lost in my ways

Fighting the feeling of being emotionally played

Due to your unresponsive ways

Walking away with my mind but my heart wants to stay

So now my mental is delayed

Needing to hear you say

Exactly what's needed to comfort me

Give me the security

In knowing you'll choose to save me in this tsunami

Winds blowing the strength out of me

Understand that I'm in a weather emergency

It's emergent that you cleared my mentality

But that's not what transpired, you see

Openly

Giving you me

Willing to accept your whole mentality

Yet, you don't see that you blinds me

What I don't know, takes my security

But you know that because of my transparency

Take it or leave it because we both know that I'm worthy

But it's ok to blame me

~U GenUis~

SUSTAINABLE

Dreaming of freedom

Release from the restraints of my mental kingdom

Seeking…searching to be free…hungering for freedom

Allowing my inner air to be free

Of the germs and chemicals around me

Breathing more clearly

Longing for my body to be free

Of outside damage…even internally

Can you imagine being free from damage

Releasing the stress that's mentally savaged

Your ways of thinking…acting because you're more than average

You were born with great courage

Making you courageously strong

No matter the hurt, pain and struggles you've undergone

Remember you are the star

Your glare should shine from afar

No matter where you are

Shining bright, bright

Even when the sun is out, the world should see a reflection of your light

Your light should even be heard to those without sight

Hearing is seeing to some, right

Pressing thru clouds like when the sun rays

Carrying a Spirit that lightens the worlds hardest days

Men, women…boys and girls

Your light is your light and this is your world   ~U GenUis~

Just Why

Why fix the body before strengthening the mind

Why ask of insight when the mental is blind

Why ask the of the amputated to take a stand

Especially when you see there's no prosthetic in hand

Why ask a person with no arms to clap

Yet, knowing that you deserve a slap

Do you ask the hurt to smile

Or do you get up and become their human towel

Do you ask for finances from the poor

Or grab them and say, " let's go to the store?"

Do you pray for healing of the sick

Or perhaps, become a beating stick

Can you see the struggle in the next person's eyes

Or play blind and sit there in disguise

How can dead grass grow

If you open the dirt and feed into the soil, that growth would overflow

~U GenUis~

Internal Joy

I don't mean to be extra but I feel I need you

Not your money, nor sex but I needed something real and true

Needing a vibe I can feel

Looking for a feeling that makes my heart heal

Taking away the years of yields

Now I'm seeing a flowery field

Where my smile is real

I sometimes wonder where will we go from here

Which sometimes brings about fear

However I'm forever grateful and sometimes shed a tear

Not one, hell… I sometimes cry

No, I'm not going to lie

I receive something more valuable from you than any money can buy

So I yearn

For you…some days my heart burn

For you…yet I desire to learn

You…yes about you, I am concerned

Although sometimes I'm a little stubborn

I thought I'd never see

The day that someone could want me for me

A man that makes me smile indefinitely

Firm but touches me so gently

That I feel loved like a newborn baby

A man that encourages me to be better

Not just desire to get my vagina wetter

A man made just for me...I can see our future together

Making memories and correcting all errors

Healing past pains

Receiving hydration through the days of rain

Being the spokesperson for each others campaign

Locking in a loyalty to mentally sustain

Yet regain

Our smiles...all while making accomplishments and popping champagne

~U GenUis~

MISTAKEN NOT DENIED

My pains hit differently, let me explain

Explain how I was a mistake but yet the one to blame

Blamed for my attitude

Yeah, I can be rude

Rude because of pains of feeling misplaced

Not knowing where I stand in this place

Beaten mentally and physically

By a sister that's supposed to protect me

Jealousy for whatever reasons, I am yet to see

Provoked into anger

Treated worse than a stranger

Seeing the man I call Dad

Treat me so bad

Bought for his other kids but left me looking sad

Mama bought L.A Gears or Jordache

That's all she had

While my sister's had Jordans and every Nike, yeah sad

Sick with my health

Yeah my dad lied about his wealth

Left me struggling, no help

But yet when his OTHER kids call, he gone step

Loosening chains

That once claimed

To be my family mane

Holding me down

While laughing at my frowns

Laughing at me like a clown

Not knowing that it was God keeping me around

~U GenUis~

12 YEARS CANCER FREE

It takes a strong will to live to be me

Trying so hard every single day to keep my sanity

Fighting thru the hurt and praying thru the pain

Never knowing is today gonna be better, worse or the same

Knowing how to love but being afraid to accept

To accept the promises God has kept

Loving those who don't love me

Yet pushing away from the ones that keep it G

Struggled my biggest battle in 2008

I swear to y'all I never thought I would see today's date

I learned a lot and experienced unthought of pains

That's what changed my entire perception of life, I'm not the same

I cry sometimes because yes I get lonely and my health play on my top too

Sometimes I wonder why me, just what did I do

So I stand my grounds and hold my head to the sky

If no one can help, I know God hears my cry

This I know because I have made it 12 years cancer FREE

And for that I give God the TOTAL victory!

~U GenUis~

I'm me!

I'm quiet with my true feelings

because I say things that make some people get offended

Others get intimidated and some get defensive

When my mouth open and the words forms

I don't mean no harm

But wait…it's straight up where I'm from

Sensitivity is sheltered

Covered by strength but However

Tough skin is forever

They key to fighting bad weather

It your best umbrella

Gaining strength

Thru any length

Willing to go to any extent

Trying not to vent

Avoiding any argument

Anger is not an action that I want to present

Being a woman at all times is my biggest intent

Holding firm as a palm tree…swallowing pain, hurt and torment

Although strength

Often make some resent

My presence but hey…I'm U GenUis…the fuck they meant

~U GenUis~

Made in the USA
Columbia, SC
03 May 2024

34904334R00035